All-Occasion
Sermon Outlines

All-Occasion Sermon Outlines

Eric W. Hayden

BAKER BOOK HOUSE
Grand Rapids, Michigan

Copyright 1978 by
Baker Book House Company
ISBN: 0-8010-4206-2
Printed in the United States of America

First printing, January 1979
Second printing, March 1980
Third printing, July 1981
Fourth printing, March 1983

Unless otherwise noted, all Scripture references are from the *King James Version*.

Other versions quoted include:
The Amplified Bible (AB)—Old Testament, copyright 1968 by Zondervan Corporation, Grand Rapids.
Good News Bible (GNB)—New Testament, copyright 1966 by American Bible Society, New York.
The Living Bible (LB), copyright 1971 by Tyndale House Publishers, Wheaton, IL.
The New English Bible (NEB), copyright 1961 by Cambridge University Press, New York
Revised Standard Version (RSV)—Old Testament, copyright 1952 by National Council of the Churches of Christ, New York.

Preface

When I began my ministry thirty years ago in a small village of some five hundred houses, my church secretary was a farmer. Knowing that I was straight from theological college (although that was preceded by six years of army service) his advice to me was: "Eric, we don't want politics or anything else that we can read about in our daily newspaper. We want something from the pulpit that we can think about when going up and down the furrows ploughing."

His advice was very sound and I have kept to it wherever I have ministered, even in the great Spurgeon's Tabernacle, London, where I ministered before and after the third rebuilding in 1959.

Having served in the armed forces, I knew the importance of doing things by numbers: "On the command *one* . . ." - "On the command *two* . . ." To keep my sermons simple and easy to remember I used divisions or points in my sermons after the style of preachers like Charles Haddon Spurgeon. I also studied, for a time, the intriguing subject of Biblical numerology, that is, the significance of certain numbers used in Scripture.

I soon came to realize that texts with numbers had a way of

sticking in people's minds, and it has been encouraging to hear, sometimes many years after the sermon was first preached, that someone remembered the text, if not much of the sermon!

Special services also fascinated me, and I soon realized their importance in attracting those who did not normally enter a church building on Sunday. Perhaps it was for that reason that I was invited to contribute to the *Baker's Dictionary of Practical Theology* on particular or special services.

In my two previous volumes of outlines I arranged my sermons in alphabetical order. In this volume I have tried to combine the simplicity of construction with numbers as an aid to memory. Of course, I am well aware that not all churches and preachers observe some of these special services, but the sermons can easily be adapted to the ordinary week-by-week teaching and evangelistic services.

As I have said before in my previous sermon outlines, these are but the bare bones, the skeletons; the reader who wishes to preach them will have to clothe them with "flesh." For this he must study the text within its context, consult good commentaries, but most of all wait in prayer on God the Holy Spirit to give him that unction, that undefinable prerequisite for all preaching.

For those readers who are not preachers, the outlines as they stand might well fill a gap in your devotional life, especially if you are ill or for some other reason housebound and so cannot attend God's house of prayer on His own day.

Eric W. Hayden

Contents

CHAPTER ONE

ZERO
The Fall of the Year (Autumn)

"There shall be no more death, neither sorrow, nor cry-ing, neither shall there be any more pain" (Rev. 21:4; cf. vv. 1, 22, 23, 25, 27).

The number *nought* in Scripture is equivalent to *nothing* or *not even one*. It is used in connection with ruins, desolation and disrepute, or with anything that has had no effect. Far from being a discouraging word, however, it is most encouraging when encountered in the last book of the Bible.

Thomas Hood, in a verse of doggerel (some may call it poetry!), writes:

> No shade, no shine, no butterflies, no bees,
> No fruits, no flowers, no leaves, no birds,—
> NOvember!

November's symbol could well be the figure *nought,* for much that we have enjoyed during the summer season has begun to fade. The autumn or fall of the year is upon us, depriving us of summer pleasures, pursuits and delights.

A similar series of *no's* or *nothings* is listed in an unusual context, that of the description of God's new heaven and earth in Revelation 21. Far from discouraging us it ought to fill us with Paul's desire and aspirations to depart this present life, since to "die is gain" and "to be with Christ is far better."

First, we must notice the location of heaven. The Russian astronauts declared that God was not there since they had not seen Him from their spacecraft. But heaven is *up* there, for Jesus Christ *ascended* after His resurrection.

John's description of heaven is simply breathtaking: jasper or translucent walls; jeweled foundations (rainbow colors); pearly gates (standing for salvation by grace); golden streets (purity); and a crystal river and a tree of life.

The dimensions are equally inspiring and intriguing: 1500 miles long and wide and the same distance high (signifying either a cube or a pyramid). In other words, the total dimensions are bigger than those of all of India!

Some biblical scholars interpret Revelation literally; others, figuratively. In either case the size is sufficient to accommodate "a number which no man can number." The context, then, is about things that are *there*; our text speaks of things that are *not there*.

I. THINGS THAT ARE NOT IN HEAVEN

A. No Sea (v. 1). Three-quarters of our present globe is sea. The sea affords us great pleasure by way of vacations spent by it and cruises taken on it. Great business (imports and exports) is conducted by way of the sea. But we cannot easily live on or under the sea. And the whole of heaven is to be habitable, for it must be able to accommodate us in the "many mansions" or abiding places.

B. No Death (v. 4). Man's last enemy, which has invaded every family for generations and has brought sorrow and solitude in its train, will be no more.

C. No Sorrow (v. 4). The sorrow brought in death's train, the sorrow caused by life's hardships and setbacks, the sorrow caused by broken friendships and marriages will be no more.

D. No Crying (v. 4). ". . . God shall wipe away all tears." The Greek word for crying implies uncontrolled sobbing. Perhaps the idea of bereavement is still in John's mind, for when "Jesus wept" the Greek implies "He burst into tears" at the graveside of Lazarus. God will be like a mother to us and wipe away all tears, for whatever reason they are flowing.

E. No Pain (v. 4). The pain that precedes death, the pain of dread diseases, the pain that follows an accident, the pains that are really heartaches—all will be dispersed without resource to modern pain-killing drugs.

F. No Temple (v. 22). There will be no specific religious structure for worship. Everywhere in heaven will be suitable for worship. Heaven will be one great temple of praise with nothing "icily regular or coldly formal" about it.

G. No Sun (v. 23). We are coming to rely on the sun more and more for heat as our other sources of fuel begin to diminish. We love its light, bathing the world in gold. But in heaven God's glory will be sufficient.

H. No Moon (v. 23). The moon reflects light from the sun. So Jesus, when on earth, came to reflect the Father. But in heaven we shall bask in the direct light of the Lamb.

I. No Night (v. 25). Eternity will be one eternal day. November reminds us of long winter nights closing in with shorter days. So our nights of ignorance, superstition and doubt will come to an end in the land of "endless day."

J. No Sin (v. 27). John says that there will be nothing that "defiles" in heaven. Think of today's pornography, immorality, greed, violence, and vice. Heaven, in contrast, will be a place of perfect purity.

What a picture! We have the opportunity to be where Christ is, to be like Him and to reign with Him! Have we made certain of our final destiny by believing in Him?

CHAPTER TWO

ONE-TENTH
Tithing or Gift Days

"Bring the full amount of your tithes to the Temple, so that there will be plenty of food there. Put me to the test and you will see that I will open the windows of heaven and pour out on you in abundance all kinds of good things" (Mal. 3:10, GNB).

Many cults are thriving today. It is said that the Mormons are the fastest-growing "church" in the world. New Mormon temples are being built everywhere. Where do these people get the necessary money in times of financial recession? *They tithe!* Should Christians, possessing the true gospel, give less than those who propagate a false religion? Should believers give less to the Lord than they give to a waiter in a restaurant or a taxicab driver as a tip or gratuity?

There are two misconceptions about tithing. Some say that tithing is an Old Testament sanction which Christians are no longer required to follow. Others say that tithing is too much of a hardship for modern Christians.

I. TITHING UNDER THE LAW OF LOVE

In Genesis 28:20, 22, we read: "And Jacob vowed a vow, saying, If God will be with me, and will keep me in this way that I go, and will give me bread to eat, and raiment to put on . . . of all that thou shalt give me I will surely give the tenth unto thee." This may have been a "foxhole promise" (like soldiers in danger in wartime). Jacob was running from Esau, but that does not deny the fact that Jacob decided on *one-tenth* long before the Mosaic law came into operation. Jacob knew what proportion God expected from him.

We can go back even further to Genesis 14:20. There we have the first case of tithing (about four hundred years before the Law). Abram had recaptured the goods of Sodom and returned them to Salem. Melchizedek, king of Salem and a priest of God, blessed Abram for giving one-tenth of the spoils in gratitude for God's help in gaining the victory—"And he gave him tithes of all."

Christians *are* under law, the new law of love. Living as we do in the "day of grace," shall we give less under grace, and motivated by love, than the Jew of old gave under his old system of law? In I Corinthians 16:2 Paul wrote: "Upon the first day of the week let every one of you lay by him in store, as God has prospered him" ("in proportion to his gains," NEB). What proportion would that be for a Jew like Paul? One-tenth! So one-tenth of the Christian's income is automatically earmarked for the Lord.

II. TITHING—MINIMUM GIVING

Tithing, even when under the Law in the Old Testament days, was only *minimum* giving and not *maximum*. Malachi insists that if God is not to be robbed, and if God's blessing is to be expected, then *all* the tithes, plus offerings, must be given to the Lord's representatives. So we begin with our obligatory minimum giving, the tithe (that could well be our regular and systematic weekly offering in church services), and then we add our thank offerings for special blessings received, such as the passing of an examination, the birth of a baby, the receiving of a legacy (and these can be devoted to special causes such as missionary societies, the world's underprivileged, Christian hospitality, and so on).

The result of such systematic giving of tithes and offerings is that it will "open the windows of heaven" and blessings will "pour out in abundance" on us and His church.

Robert Laidlaw of New Zealand testified to this again and again. When he was converted at eighteen years of age, he promised to give one-tenth to God. Two years later he increased his giving to 15 percent of his income; then 20 percent, then 25 percent. At the age of twenty-five he was giving 50 percent of his income to God, and at the age of seventy he testified to the way God had blessed him throughout his life, both spiritually and materially.

Without such a basis as one-tenth our giving becomes slipshod and haphazard and Paul urges that "everything be done decently and in order." So let us remember that God's Word teaches: "The tenth is holy unto the Lord." Someone has put it: "Give less than a tenth and be a thief; give a tenth and be a Pharisee; give more than a tenth and be a Christian!"

There is one infallible test we can apply to assess our giving: If God gave me ten times what I give to Him, could I live on it? Many of us would experience great difficulty indeed.

Finally, all our giving should be looked at not in the light of fractions or percentages but in the light of the Lord's giving:

"[He] loved me, and gave himself for me" (Gal. 2:20). He gave His all on Calvary, holding nothing back. It was a reflection of His Father's giving: "God so loved the world *that He gave . . .*" (John 3:16). God gave His best and His all, His only Son. No wonder the apostle Paul described this divine gift as God's "unspeakable gift," a gift that surpasses human eloquence to describe.

A tax inspector once visited a church and asked for a conducted tour. At the end of it he seemed quite disappointed. When the clergyman asked why, he was told: "Well, from the tax returns of your members I thought the aisles would be paved with gold, for the members have included so many deductions for charitable gifts on their tax forms."

Is the spiritual revival we need withheld because of the way Christians withhold their material wealth?

CHAPTER THREE

ONE

Youth Service

"And no one can ever lay any other real foundation than that one we already have—Jesus Christ" (I Cor. 3:11, LB).

Jesus Christ made many claims for Himself. Some of them are summed up in what we refer to as the seven *I AMs*. Besides these He claimed for Himself a unique birth and relationship to God. These claims were supported by friends and foes alike. His deeds supported His words. Not only did no other man speak as He spoke, but no one else was able to do similar miracles.

Many New Testament writers, among them the apostle Paul, have stressed the claims of Christ on our lives. Paul responded to the claim of Christ on his life, as did his many converts (the Philippian jailor, Lydia the business woman). Outside the Bible era, people like Wesley, Whitefield, C. H.

Spurgeon and later, C. S. Lewis, C. E. Joan and Malcolm Muggeridge have testified to the transformation that Christ, through the Holy Spirit, wrought in their lives.

In our text Paul is emphasizing that Christ is for everyone who wants a true and proper foundation in his life. This refers especially to young people searching for a solid base upon which to build their future.

The text begins with "for," a backward-looking word, reminding us that the apostle has been writing about a master-builder or architect. Like an architect he knows that the substructure determines the final superstructure.

I. FOUNDATIONS ARE FUNDAMENTAL

Good schooling, a good college or university education provides a foundation for a future career. At school we quickly discover that simple multiplication tables provide the foundation for complicated calculations. Simple scales and five-finger exercises on the piano are the foundation for playing Bach and Beethoven at a later stage.

Foundations, then, are fundamental. An architect or builder can leave out windows in a building, but he cannot leave out the foundation.

II. NO SUPERSTRUCTURE IF NO SUBSTRUCTURE

We cannot build up if we do not first go down. The builders have first to go down through yielding topsoil and clay until they have something more solid upon which to lay a foundation. Our Lord pointed out that a house built on shifting sand would fall in a flood, whereas a house built on rock would stand firm.

This substructure determines three things about a building:

A. Its Size. The building's final dimensions are determined by the pegged-out foundations.

B. Its Shape. The building will be square, oblong, round or rectangular, according to the shape or design of the foundations.

C. Its Stability. Since buildings are vertical, foundations have to be horizontal to provide stability.

III. JESUS CHRIST IS THE ONE AND ONLY SUBSTRUCTURE

Christ is the only true foundation upon which to build a life that is safe, secure and satisfying. He alone can determine the size, shape and stability of a young person's life. Pleasure, materialism, politics—the modern *gods* of twentieth-century society—do not provide an adequate foundation for a young person's life. We need the foundation that is already laid, Jesus Christ.

The architect watches the foundation of a building very carefully when it is laid. He looks to see that the workmen are going down to the right depth. He watches to see that the concrete is mixed without "plums" (inferior, breakable ashes instead of true hard-core). Jesus Christ, being God's own Son, being truly man and God, is the one and only true foundation on which to build Christian character.

The young person who accepts Christ as Savior, and follows His example and teaching, will be building on the best foundation for the future. His life will be such a building that there will be fewer weaknesses, such as immorality, deception, underhandedness. The size of such a life will be full stature. To be a mature man or woman in Christ is God's original intention for all of us. The shape of the life will be "all things new" or "new creations." The Holy Spirit will make us change "from one degree of glory to another," so that we become more and more like our Savior. And the stability of the life will be: "Neither shall any man pluck them out of my hand. . . . [nor] out of my Father's hand." We shall be doubly secure and shall be able to sing:

> On Christ the solid Rock I stand
> All other ground is shifting sand.

Let us get our priorities right: first the substructure, then the superstructure; first the foundation, then the building. We don't begin at the top but at the bottom, humbly confessing our sin at the foot of the cross, then trusting the Christ of Calvary for eternal salvation.

CHAPTER FOUR

ONE
Men's Sunday

"The younger son gathered all together, and took his journey into a far country..." (Luke 15:13).

Jesus began His parable by saying: "A certain man had *two* sons," and in a sense there are two prodigals in the parable. One was a backslider by going away from home; the other was a backslider who remained at home (just as there are spiritual backsliders within the church today).

Others say that it is really a parable about the *father* rather than about a son or two sons, for it is the father's love and forgiveness that is so prominent.

However, it has long been known as "The Parable of the Prodigal Son," but the younger son can hardly be studied without reference to his brother and his father.

There is a very simple way by which to remember the career of the younger son: home, sick of home, homesick, home again! This is often the career of young men (and perhaps just as frequently, young women) in this twentieth century, with lack of love and discipline in the home and the attractions of the materialistic world outside.

I. HOME

The old song expresses this well-worn sentiment: "Be it ever so humble, there's no place like home." The word *home* takes up many columns of print in any dictionary of quotations. It stands for:

A. Safety. The young child grows up in a home (if it is a good home) that keeps him safe against the world and want.

B. Security. Mother and father endeavor to provide a situation within the home that gives a feeling of security to their offspring.

C. Comfort. Parents try to provide comfortable surroundings for their children, not, if the parents are wise, protecting in an artificial environment in contrast with the world of "hard knocks" outside.

D. Companionship. Responsible parents endeavor to be friends and companions, as well as a mother and father, to their children. They encourage their children to bring their friends home and share in the hospitality and family atmosphere.

When God created man, He made him for home and family life. In the Garden of Eden Adam and Eve experienced companionship with God as He walked and talked with them in the cool of the evening.

II. SICK OF HOME

A true home, as we have seen, must have a certain amount of discipline. This gives young people a sense of security, whereas being brought up without any rules and regulations leaves them with a feeling of insecurity.

A small boy packed his bag to run away from home. After going through the front gate, he returned. His young sister said, "Have you forgotten something?" "No!" he replied, "I want mommy to run away with me."

In our Lord's parable there were several stages in the prodigal's leaving home:

A. Note His Preparations. He asked for money, the future inheritance he would have received when his father died.

B. He Did Not Delay—"not many days after." Like the gambler with his winnings he was eager to be off to spend his money on pleasurable living.

C. God Stepped In. When he had spent all, when he had become penniless and friendless, when he had an empty stomach, then he heard God speaking to him.

So it is with the spiritual backslider. On our downward path God speaks through various means and in various ways.

III. HOMESICK

Memories were awakened—"he came to himself" or to his senses. He realized he had been mad to run away.

Not sure of the reception he still made plans to return and thought of words with which to placate his father. The flashy friends, fast living and bright lights now did not mean as much to him as the comforts of the home he had left.

IV. HOME AGAIN!

Did he walk, hitch a ride, beg food? We are not told. In our imagination we can picture his arrival.

A. The Hilltop. Walking up the last hilltop of his journey back he saw the old homestead in the distance. He saw his elder brother and the farm hands going about their business.

B. The Rooftop. On the flat eastern roof the father had kept a daily vigil. Perhaps his sight was going dim or tears formed a film, but soon he saw the familiar figure of his lost son.

C. The Slowness of the Son. He was weak and weary; he was half-afraid of the reception he would receive.

D. The Swiftness of the Father. Forgetting age and dignity he ran down the outside staircase of an eastern home, two steps at a time, and embraced his son.

The son repented; the father forgave and then because actions speak louder than words, he gave his son gifts—a ring for assurance; sandals that spoke of liberty; a robe that spoke of security; a feast and merry-making to remind him of the true pleasures of home.

We live in a woman's world, we are told. We are unisex. We are all equal. Without a doubt mothers play a great part in homemaking, but the father must exercise loving discipline; and if a son ''goes over the traces'' the father must be as ready to receive him back as God in Christ is ready to welcome the son who has strayed away from spiritual things and whose love has grown cold.

CHAPTER FIVE

ONE
Youth Service

"Go . . . sell . . . give . . . come . . . take . . . follow . . ."
(Mark 10:21).

These six words taken from our text sum up the Savior's suggestive commands to a young person who had "one thing missing" ("One thing thou lackest," KJV; "You need only one thing," GNB).

Note that the Savior has given the young man six *positive* things to do after previously reminding him of the *negatives* of the Law ("Do *not* commit adultery," v. 19, etc.). A negative religion is a joyless religion; a Christian faith founded upon positives is a religion that is happy and blessed.

There are many today like this rich young ruler who want something more than money can buy. Luxuries, pleasures and possessions do not always bring happiness. The stars of stage, screen (cinema and television), the famous of the "pop" music world—many of these people are not really happy and suicides are not unknown among them.

How earnest the young man was! He came *running* (v. 17) to Jesus. The psychologists tell us that we run from fear or fight fear (flight or fight). But this young man was running *to* not *away from*. He was running to the One who had the secret of happiness.

He not only ran, he *knelt*. This again showed his earnestness (as well as his humility), for it was the sign that he was going to beseech the Savior. He was morally good: he kept, and had obeyed all the commandments, as far as he was able, from the days of his youth onwards.

No wonder Jesus loved him, for people do not usually want to keep His Father's commands. But He loved him so much that He substituted six other commands for the commands of the decalogue.

I. GO

This word implied *direction*. Many young people are looking for direction today. They feel a need to be pointed in the right direction. Because their parents seem to have lost all sense of direction they turn to the "meditation experts," the scientists, the politicians, the educationalists, but all in vain. None of these has the answer to being lost spiritually. Drugs may help for a time, the "trips" helping them to forget the dead ends or cul-de-sacs of everyday living. Only Jesus Christ has the authoritative word: "This is the way, walk in it," because He *is* the Way, the Truth and the Life.

II. SELL

This was Christ's word of *relinquishment* to the young man. He was not asked to give away his profits from his investments (his tithe perhaps), he was asked to give all his possessions away, for they were a hindrance to happiness. That does not mean all must become poor to become proper Christians. God has used the riches of many financially influential Christians to extend His kingdom at home and overseas. It is not *money* that is wrong, it is "the *love* of money that is the root of all evil." Riches were this young man's downfall; they were a deterrent or drawback to him in taking the right direction.

Sometimes it is not money that we must relinquish to become followers of Christ but a habit or hobby, a pleasure or possession.

III. GIVE

This is a step further than relinquishment; this is a call to *sacrifice*. The relinquishment had to be complete. He could have relinquished his possessions by selling them—*at a profit!* He was not to *sell* but to *give*. Often we have to sacrifice to become Christians. Christ's call is to "take up the cross daily" to become a disciple. The cross is the mark of sacrifice. It was on a cross that He was soon to make the supreme sacrifice for this rich young ruler and all who are like him.

IV. COME

This word was often on the lips of the Savior, for it is the word of *invitation*. *Come*, now, *come* one and all, *come* in whatever condition you are—these were the ways Christ used this lovely word. Nothing need deter us or delay us; we can come at any time.

V. TAKE

This is the word of *reception*. We receive the cross that we must carry as a sign that we belong to Christ. We talk too glibly about our "crosses," the illnesses and infirmities that we have to bear or put up with. They must all be looked at in the light of Christ's suffering on the cross of Calvary. Then we shall be able to sing:

> "Take up thy cross," the Savior said,
> "If thou would'st My disciple be;
> Take up thy cross, *with willing heart*,
> And humbly follow after Me."

VI. FOLLOW

This is *identification*. We not only bear a cross like Christ's, but we live daily becoming more like Him, identifying ourselves with His will and purpose for the world—the saving of our friends and neighbors.

These six challenging words are followed by three tragic ones: he "went away grieved." He came for eternal life and went away without it. He kept his riches, but he lost God's real treasure.

CHAPTER SIX

ONE PLUS ONE
Missionary Sunday

"Very much land still remains to be possessed" (Josh. 13:1, AB).

In the previous chapter Joshua had been doing a very simple sum in arithmetic, adding one to one to one until the sum total reached thirty-one. He did not need a computer or pocket calculator for such a simple sum. In actual fact he was cataloging his conquests—a typical habit when one begins to feel the weight of advancing years! Joshua is described as "old and stricken in years" ("Joshua was now an old man," LB).

Having won his laurels and proved his prowess, he now looks back with complacency. No wonder God speaks plainly and says, ". . . there remaineth yet very much land to be possessed."

Joshua as a general had gained much territory, but there

was still more to be conquered. This was no time for simple sums but for taking stock and going forward into battle for the Lord.

There are in these words three calls from God to Joshua:

I. FROM COMPLACENCY TO DISSATISFACTION

The English language has several vivid expressions to describe the complacent person: he "blows his own trumpet," "pats himself on the back," or "shakes hands with himself." One needs to be a contortionist to do all three at once! But Joshua was revealing his complacency by this exercise in simple arithmetic.

Perhaps Joshua, like many great generals, had little sense of humor. War is serious business; there is not much to laugh at. But Joshua could not even raise a smile at himself.

"Laugh and grow fat" is an old proverb. Doctors now affirm that it should be, "Laugh and grow *fit*." Hearty laughter helps tone up certain muscles. So if Joshua had taken a more light-hearted look at his past victories he might have been more venturesome for the future, without a divine reprimand.

In the same way, as we read of the history of Christian missions, of the founding of our missionary societies and of thrilling missionary lives, we should not be complacent but courageous. We should be filled with a holy desire to outstrip our forefathers in the faith.

George Grenfell came out of the hardware trade to found a chain of mission stations across Africa. Gladys Aylward left a life of "service" (servant in a large family) in London to go to China and lead a large number of children to safety.

We should not be adding up our "ones" but saying with C. T. Studd: "The evangelization of the world in our generation." It is not Luther—1; Spurgeon—2; Wesley—3; Billy

Graham—4; it is, what can *I* do or my church do to continue extending God's kingdom, for "very much land still remains to be possessed."

II. FROM APATHY TO IMMEDIATE ACTION

Joshua worked out his sum, cross-checked it, labeled it as correct—perhaps even had it audited! But he had forgotten the sum God had given him (Joshua 12:2–6). Joshua had not completed his commission; he had become apathetic. Now the call of God comes a second time (as it did later to Jonah) to be up and doing.

Joshua's fault was that he put length of service on the credit side instead of the debit side. We all tend to do this with advancing age. "I have served as a Sunday school teacher or a preacher for twenty, thirty, forty years," we say, looking backward like Joshua. Against that we must put our text and the words of the apostle Paul, that we are to be "always abounding in the work of the Lord."

"You are not dangerously *ill*," said a doctor to a patient, "but dangerously *old*." There is no time to be lost for the Christian. We are becoming dangerously old; the world will one day be "folded up like a garment"; night is coming "when no man can work." We must rouse ourselves to immediate action for "very much land still remains to be possessed."

III. FROM SLEEP TO SPIRITUAL AWAKENING

Look back to your conversion. Did you not promise to serve Him to the end? Now perhaps the fire has burned low in the hearth of your heart. You may be asking, "Where is the blessedness I knew?" If that is your condition, then be like William Carey, the "father of modern missions." It is said of him: "The disappointments of God surged through his soul, and he cried out, 'Is nothing to be done then?' '' And when he realized at that early meeting of ministers that nothing was going to be done, *he went and did it*! He made a leather globe, a map of the world sewed together with pieces of leather from his shoemaker's trade. Then he looked at the various countries, crying over them, ''Pagan, pagan, pagan.''

So we must be reawakened to the needs of the world, taking an atlas, if need be, and crying over those in Communist lands who are denied the gospel; crying over those in the materialistic West who are blinded by affluence.

But renewed prayer is not sufficient. It has been said that we cannot serve God with our fingertips. The Bible says: ''Whatsoever your *hand* finds to do, do it with all your might.'' It might mean to dig deep into pocket or purse; it might mean to train underdeveloped peoples in the use of modern machinery; it might mean to point others to Christ by preaching or through the distribution of Christian literature. There are a hundred-and-*one* ways of claiming the unpossessed for Christ. Listen to the divine call for the unpossessed.

CHAPTER SEVEN

TWO

An Evangelistic Service

The figure *two* occurs in a good many proverbial sayings: "Two's company, three's a crowd"; "It takes two to make a quarrel," and so on. As children it was quite a feat to be able to say, "I now know my two-times table." Two was a figure that Jesus Christ used frequently during the days of His earthly ministry:

I. TWO KINDS OF PEOPLE

In Matthew 25:31–33, He spoke of people as being like either sheep or goats. He was describing the day of judgment and likening it to a great separation, the sheep on His right hand and the goats on His left. He was speaking of the saved and the lost.

To put His picture into modern form we must imagine a great crowd in a sports arena. Suddenly there is a great division—not into supporters of opposing teams, not into families, not into nationalities, but a division into Christian and non-Christian.

We are, of course, divided now—by Calvary. Either we have responded to the love of the God-Man who died on the cross for us, or we have rejected Him. The two thieves represent us all. One repented, and one continued to revile.

II. TWO FATHERS

We sometimes talk glibly of "the Fatherhood of God and the brotherhood of man." God is the *Creator* of all men but not the *Father* of all. Jesus said in John 8:42, 44: " . . . If God were your Father, you would love me . . . ye are of your father the devil." God becomes our Father only when we believe on His Son and become one of His adopted sons and daughters. Until that moment of belief, following our sincere repentance for our sins, the devil is our father.

How does God become our Father? "No man comes to the Father but by me," said Jesus. When His disciples asked Him, "Show us the Father," His reply was, "Do you not know Me?" It was by belief in the Son that they could know the Father.

III. ONLY TWO WAYS

In the Sermon on the Mount (Matthew 7:13, 14), Jesus said: "Enter ye in at the strait gate: for wide is the gate and broad is the way that leadeth to destruction, and many there be which go in thereat: Because strait is the gate and narrow is the way which leadeth unto life, and few there be that find it."

There are only two roads to choose through life: one that leads to further life, eternal life, and one that leads to death, spiritual death.

That is true of life in general. We can take an easy road through college, getting by with low grades, or we can be diligent students aiming for the highest. We can be mere dabblers in some hobby or we can become absorbed in it, passionate about it. We can become average pianists or we can practice and practice until we are more proficient. Genius has been defined as "the infinite capacity for taking pains."

Two ways, and Jesus said, "*I am* the way." He points along the rugged, blood-stained path up the green hill of Calvary and says, "This is the way; you walk in it."

IV. TWO FUTURES

Once more Jesus spoke of the day of judgment when God will say, "Come, ye blessed" or, "Depart . . . ye cursed" (Matt. 25:34, 41).

What alternatives! Either we inherit a kingdom prepared for us (even now being prepared for us by Jesus Himself!), or we go into everlasting punishment. And these alternatives were spoken of by the "meek and lowly" Jesus, not some "hell-fire preacher" as he would be termed today.

Some say our Lord was using picture language. Even if He were, the picture must represent something just as severe as "everlasting fire," and something just as sublime as "the kingdom prepared for you."

V. TWO DEATHS

"It is appointed unto man once to die . . ." says the writer of the Letter to the Hebrews, but he is referring only to physical death that results in the soul being separated from the body. Later will come the day of judgment that Jesus spoke about, and then the unsaved will be sentenced to their "second death" (Rev. 20:14).

Scripture is very silent about this second death and we should not try to go beyond the bounds God has set up. We can assume that it is a terrible state in which there seems to be no second chance of responding to the claims of Christ. So before we "shuffle off this mortal coil" (as Shakespeare put it), we should choose eternal life and so escape the second death.

Two kinds of people—which are you? *Two* fathers—which is yours? *Two* roads—on which one are you? *Two* futures—which is yours? *Two* deaths—or will you experience only the first which will be the gateway to eternity?

CHAPTER EIGHT

THREE
A Christmas Service

"[Wise men] worshipped him . . . and presented unto him gifts" (Matt. 2:1, 11).

Christmas cards are not always Scriptural! They often show three *kings*; the Bible tells us they were Wise Men or astrologers. They depict *three* kings; we are only told they presented three kinds of gifts. Usually the setting is the manger, whereas Scripture tells us that the end of their search was the "house" where "the young child was."

Their guiding sign is truthfully portrayed on our Christmas cards and friezes: they followed a star. In those days men had no compasses or radar. They did not follow the Pole Star or Southern Cross like sailors; they had God's special star to guide them, a new star that heralded the birth of an important person. Twentieth-century scientists now believe that such a star appeared in the heavens at the very time indicated by Scripture.

The goal of their search is also indicated on our cards and other Christmas decorations—the Lord Jesus Christ, Immanuel, God-with-us. They came not to worship Mary. Joseph was only an indication of our Lord's humanity as well as divinity (the result of the Virgin Birth). Their real goal was Jesus Himself. Caesar "came, saw and conquered." These wise men came, saw, worshiped, gave and then returned with the good news.

There are two important sets of questions to ask ourselves regarding the story of the Wise Men. One set has to do with the Wise Men themselves; the other is concerned with the Savior whom they sought.

I. QUESTIONS ABOUT THE WISE MEN

A. Who Were They? Some call them "Magi." The term is misleading in that it makes us think of magicians! They were astrologers. (In the modern sense they were astronomers—students of the heavenly bodies, rather than sooth-sayers, fortune-tellers, writers of horoscopes.) They were philosophers and interpreters of dreams. Theirs was an honorable profession.

B. Where Did They Come From? The Bible tells us that they came from the "east." The Old Testament speaks of "wise men of Babylon." The nature of their gifts—gold, frankincense and myrrh—perhaps as much as anything indicates their home.

C. When Did They Come? They arrived when Jesus was in a "house" and nearly two years old (the age at which the king decreed infant males should be slaughtered). That is why the Wise Men asked, "Where is he that *was* born" . . . , that is, "has been born some time ago," not "born this very day," as the shepherds acknowledged. If they came from Babylon their journey was approximately six hundred miles and would have taken at least six weeks. If they had arrived one or even two days earlier, the forty days of "purification" would not have been up, and Joseph and Mary could not have fled to escape the massacre. If they had arrived one or two days later, the family would have already left for Jerusalem and then Nazareth. God's timetable was as exact at Jesus' birth as it was at His death, when Simon of Cyrene arrived on the scene at the right moment to carry the cross.

D. What Presents Did They Bring? They brought gold to acknowledge that He was king; frankincense to acknowledge His priesthood (used in the tabernacle and temple as incense); and myrrh, which was used in embalming bodies, to acknowledge His humanity—a prophet, a preacher and teacher. They brought three gifts to emphasize that he had a three-fold office: prophet, priest and king.

II. QUESTIONS ABOUT THE SAVIOR

A. Where Can We Find Him Today? This is the most important of the questions. We have no star in the heavens, but we have the Scriptures, the Holy Spirit, the preached message of salvation by Sunday school teacher, pastor or evangelist.

B. How Can We Find Him Today? We can find Him by following our "sign" and then looking within at our own sinful hearts, realizing our dire need of Him. The Wise Men admitted their ignorance by asking along the route. We must have the same desire as Job: "Oh, that I knew where I might find Him!" No longer do we go to a crib but to a cross. The baby of Bethlehem grew to be the man of Calvary.

C. When Can We Find Him Today? The Wise Men found Him *as soon as they could*! They did not linger on the way. They did not wait until He had grown up and become a man.

The sooner the better is the correct time, for to delay may be too late. *Now* is the accepted time; *now* is the day of salvation. The Holy Spirit "will not always strive with man." So find Him while you feel the influence of the Holy Spirit at work in your life. One day He who came to earth the first time at Christmas is to come a second time, and then it will be too late to find Him as Savior, for He will come as Judge.

D. What Do We Do When We Find Him Today? The Wise Men fell down, probably awestruck at His beauty. They also fell down in the sense of humility in worship. For us, too, He is "the altogether lovely One." So he deserves our worship, having died to save us. The Wise Men presented their gifts. We, too, must give Him a gift: first ourselves, and then all that we are and have. Nothing less than total surrender will do for the King of kings and Lord of lords.

CHAPTER NINE

FIVE

Hospital or Medical Missions Sunday

"Near the Sheep Gate in Jerusalem there is a pool with five porches" (John 5:2, GNB).

It is possible to study this amazing incident from several angles: the doctor, the patient, the disease, the treatment or the hospital (the latter being called "Christ's Hospital" by C. H. Spurgeon).

If we look at the hospital we notice that it had five porches or alcoves. We may liken these to five typical wards in a modern hospital.

I. THE SURGICAL WARD

Surgical means "to cure by manual operation as opposed to medicine or drugs," according to the dictionary. In surgery the "knife" is used, and sometimes it has to cut deep to deal with the root cause of the disease. This is not as painful today, with the techniques of modern surgery, as it was before the days of anesthetics (discovered by a Christian, remember!).

God has to deal drastically with the disease the Bible calls *sin*. First He calls attention to it through the convicting power of the Holy Spirit. Often this conviction is as painful as the disease, for sometimes He uses illness, bereavement, trial, or affliction to bring us to our senses regarding His holiness and our sinfulness.

Then the "knife" is used. Scripture becomes "quick and powerful, sharper than any two-edged sword, piercing even to the dividing asunder of soul and spirit, and of the joints and marrow, and is a discerner of the thoughts and intents of the heart." As we read it, or hear it expounded, the Word of God does its own work and deals with our sin.

There was once an old doctor who was nicknamed "Dr. My Book," for he was always recommending to his patients the book he had written! God has written a Book that deals with sin and its cure. We need to read it and believe it, saying to ourselves, "God said it, I believe it, that settles it."

The most drastic surgery for sin, however, was the cross of Calvary. Only the death of God's own Son could really and finally deal with sin, its power and its penalty.

II. THE MEDICAL WARD

Treatment by medicine is not as feared by most people as surgery. There are two kinds of medicine in God's "drug cabinet": blood-red and colorless. The first is described by John in his first letter: "The blood of Jesus Christ, God's Son, cleanses us from all sin." Once again we are made to think of Calvary and the blood that flowed from the Savior's five wounds.

The colorless liquid is the water described in John's Gospel: "The water that I shall give him shall be in him a well of water springing up into everlasting life." This stands for the unfailing supply of God's saving grace.

"Three times a day," the doctor writes on our prescriptions. We need take God's remedy only once, for He who saves can also keep us in the faith: "kept by the power of God, through faith" (I Peter 1:5). Faith saves us, and faith keeps us. "Once saved, always saved" is the simple summing up of one of the five points of Calvinism called "The Perseverance of the Saints."

III. THE CHILDREN'S WARD

The children's ward is not the maternity ward where babies are born; it is the children's ward where repentant believers have been "born again." Jesus once said, "Except you become as little children you cannot enter the kingdom of heaven."

It is not being born in a Christian country or a Christian home which saves us. ("Being born in a garage does not make one an automobile"—Billy Graham.) What saves us is being born from above by the Spirit of God, a supernatural, miraculous act of God through His regenerating Spirit.

IV. THE SPECIALIST'S WARD

A specialist is a man who is devoted to one particular part of the human anatomy. There are many kinds of specialists, including ear, nose, throat and eye specialists.

Jesus Christ is the great Heart Specialist. "Out of the heart . . . ," Jesus said, "all kinds of sin proceed." But He can perform a spiritual "heart transplant": "A new heart will I give you . . . I will take away your heart of stone and give you a heart of flesh." All we need to do is pray, "Create in me, Oh, God, a clean heart."

V. THE RECEPTION DESK

This is where we go first on arrival at the hospital. The details of our visit must be written down—time of arrival and admission; recommendation by the doctor; and then the escort takes care of us and directs us to the appropriate ward. If, however, we have an accident or severe illness, then we are brought to the emergency room by ambulance and taken by stretcher directly to the appropriate treatment area.

We should not delay. The doors of "Mercy Hospital" (Bethesda—House of Mercy) are open day and night. The "staff" is always in attendance, on perpetual duty. If we do not come in time for healing, then we shall end up in the mortuary, for "the wages of sin is death," and "the soul that sins shall die."

Paraphrase John 5:2 to fit your own situation:

"Now there is at (your town or city's name), close by (insert your address), a church (write in the name of your church) having five porches." Then in your imagination enter into the appropriate ward for healing, for spiritual wholeness. The great Heart Specialist is waiting to receive you and restore you.

TEN

A Wedding Service

"... What woman having ten pieces of silver, if she lose one piece, does not light a candle, and sweep the house, and seek diligently till she find it?" (Luke 15:8).

Most commentators are agreed that the woman's lost piece of silver was part of her wedding dowry, a coin strung like a necklace but hanging round her forehead. They are also agreed that the woman represents the church, as in Paul's picture of the bride and groom. Dr. G. Campbell Morgan writes: "The woman is the type of the Spirit's operation through the church ... the first reference to the Holy Spirit in the Bible suggests Motherhood." C. H. Spurgeon comments: "This parable represents the work of the Holy Spirit in and through the church. The church is evermore represented as a woman, either the chaste bride of Christ, or the shameless courtesan of Babylon. The church is most fitly set forth as a woman."

Paul, of course, draws a parallel between the bride and groom, the church and the intimate marriage relationship of a man and his wife. As the woman's lost piece of silver was dear to her, so the church is precious to the Head of the church, as precious as the wife is to the husband.

There are three stages in the parable: the coin was lost, looked for and then found. In the same way there are various stages in courtship and marriage.

I. THE COIN WAS LOST

Whether the clasp was weak, or the joint between this piece of silver and the next was broken while she was doing housework, we are not told. So there are various ways in which a loving relationship in marriage can be lost, through inconsiderate ways, through noncommunication, and so on.

It was lost in the dust of the floor. Some marriages are dragged down to the dust in the divorce courts today. It was lost but not forgotten. So when a marriage begins to break up it is helpful to remember the good times in the past. It was lost but still claimed—"*my* piece which was lost." So "whom God has joined together, let no man put asunder." The marriage bond is really indissoluble.

The silver coin was also valued highly, otherwise she would not have gone to such lengths to find it. So we should go to great lengths to keep the early "bloom" of married life. Thankfully the coin was not lost hopelessly. The woman did not despair of finding it. She set to work at once to find it. No marriage is lost hopelessly either. Under God it can become a new thing and not just "patched up."

II. THE COIN WAS LOOKED FOR

It was looked for personally. Marriage and guidance counselors, pastors, even family doctors can be helpful when things go wrong with a marriage, but we ourselves must also be prepared to do our part to make a marriage work.

Looking for the lost coin was a matter of chief concern for this woman. She stopped everything else in order to find it. In our world of broken marriages, easy divorces, wife-swapping and the general lowering of moral standards, we should make it our chief concern to keep our ideals for a Christian marriage.

The woman used proper aids for finding her coin. She lit a candle. So we must rely upon prayer (the family that prays together, stays together) and the family altar to cement our marriage relationship.

She became engrossed in her search. With her candle and broom she forgot her other housework, her needlework and all the rest, and busied herself in finding her lost piece of silver. Marriage is not a part-time occupation. We must become engrossed in each other and in striving to see that we lose none of the things that first brought us together.

This woman persevered until she found it. Never give up! Keep at it! Each day seek the help of the Holy Spirit so that your marriage may be enduring and thus a testimony to unbelieving friends and acquaintances.

III. THE COIN WAS FOUND

The result was two-fold: First she herself rejoiced, then she called her friends and neighbors in, and they rejoiced with her.

All her time, trouble and perseverance were rewarded. She

had found what she was looking for. So it is in marriage. There is no joy (except the joy of salvation—"joy in the presence of the angels of God over one sinner that repents") like that happiness experienced by a married couple who have found each other to be all that they expected.

And what a testimony this is to neighbors and friends. How some of them will envy us! How many of them will rejoice for us as they see our happiness in each other's company! There will be joy in our hearts, joy in our home, joy in our neighborhood, when we are truly united in the bonds of Christian love. This is one of the most practical ways of testifying to the power of Christ in our lives. When we show to the world what He can do for us as man and wife, it is better than a hundred sermons. Neighbors and friends will see that Christ is the head of this house, the unseen guest at every meal, the silent listener to every conversation. Then they will take notice and be the more receptive to our message that, as lost pieces of silver, they too are being looked for by God Himself who loves them and perseveres until He finds them. He used a candle, the Light of the world, His own Son, nearly two thousand years ago, in order to find us.

CHAPTER ELEVEN

THREE HUNDRED
Men's Sunday

"... By the three hundred men that lapped will I save you ..." (Judg. 7:7).

This text has been called "the death warrant to statistics." However carefully we calculate or computerize our statistics, they are as nothing to God. He is interested in quality not quantity. He reduced 32,000 men to 300 in order to bring about a glorious victory and to bring glory to His name.

This old story is still up-to-date, for it emphasizes that God always has His man for the hour: Gideon, Samson, Paul, Wesley, Calvin, Luther, Billy Graham.

From the context we see that God's people were being oppressed by the Midianites. They had to live in caves, and even their leader had to do things by night, under cover of darkness. Before he could lead them to victory after seven years of oppression he had to expel worldliness and idolatry, doubt and indifference. Then with 300 men he was able to conquer the Midianites.

This thrilling story is best considered in two parts: a time of trial, followed by a time of triumph.

I. THE TIME OF TRIAL

First, their *courage* was being tested. They were in a fearful state. Twenty-two thousand men had left their ranks, and this depletion sapped their courage. They were, however, better off without them.

A clergyman once asked a brother in the ministry: "Have you had any new additions to your church lately?" The reply was: "No, but we have had some glorious deductions!" Sometimes deductions are necessary because God does not work through big batallions but through a chosen few, a remnant or even a baby as at Bethlehem on the first Christmas.

Next, their *caution* was being tested. Gideon was to command an army of 300 men that "lapped." This meant that some of the men would kneel down, put their mouths close to the water and use both hands to scoop it in. Others, more cautious, would only kneel down, scoop up the water in one hand, keeping their sword hand ready for drawing their sword from its scabbard. They would lap the water from the palm of one hand. So the Christian is to *watch* as well as pray.

Their *loyalty* was also being tested. These 300 men did not know one another very well. They did not know Gideon very well. They had never fought together under his command. They had to remember that their real leader and captain was God Himself. So it is with us—"our sufficiency is of God."

Jabez Bunting, an old Methodist preacher, read the words, "I can do all things . . . Paul that's a lie! I can do all things . . . Paul that's a monstrous lie. I can do all things, *through Christ who strengthens me*—Oh, I beg your pardon Paul, that makes all the difference." So they had God on their side (one with God is a majority), as well as Gideon.

And their *weapons* were being tested. They were accustomed to the sling, the bow and the spear. Now they were to rely on torches hidden in earthenware pitchers! So today our weapons are being tested. We are not to rely on our visual aids, our films and tape-recordings; these are only *aids*. Our real weapon is "the foolishness of preaching"—that is what saves men.

II. THE TIME OF TRIUMPH

It was a two-fold triumph, a triumph of methods and results.

Look at the triumph of *methods*. Their weapons were unique. First they were issued torches. These surely stand for the believer's witness by the kind of life he lives. Writing to the Philippians the apostle Paul said: "In the midst of a crooked and perverse nation, among whom you shine as lights in the world."

The torches were hidden beneath upturned pitchers or large jars. This surely stands for the Holy Spirit at work in the believer's life and reminds us of Paul writing to the Corinthians: " . . . We have this treasure in earthen vessels, that the excellency of the power may be of God, and not of us" (II Cor. 4:7).

Finally, they each had a trumpet. This was not a surprise weapon but one that had been long neglected. Yet it was required by Levitical law. Note that it was a trumpet and not a tin whistle! "Let the redeemed *say* so." The torch was a reminder that our daily life should be a testimony to the world. The trumpet tells us that our lips must also be eloquent. It reminds us of the Jubilee trumpet, blown during the Year of Release. Our message to the world is that we can be released from the bondage of Satan and sin. "If the Son . . . shall make you free, ye shall be free indeed" (John 8:36).

What a triumph of *results*! There was no rush, no panic. They stood still and watched God at work. They broke the jars, the light shone out, the trumpet sounded; and then could be written the shortest military dispatch on record: They "ran, and cried, and fled" (Judg. 7:21). It was an utter rout.

Are you one of the 300? A missionary in Shanghai with one finger typed the complete Wenli Bible—he was one of the 300. Frances Ridley Havergal, the invalid hymnwriter—she was one of the 300. "Quit you like men," urges the apostle Paul. We may not be able to translate the Bible, compose hymns or tunes, stand in a pulpit and preach, but we can do the one thing for which God has given us a talent. "Stir up" or "fan into a flame" the "gift that is within you," wrote Paul. After asking for a revelation of God's will and the replenishment of the Holy Spirit that we may have His enabling power within us, we can give our best to God.

CHAPTER TWELVE

THREE THOUSAND
Church Anniversary

"... About three thousand in all ... joined with the other believers in regular attendance at the apostles' teaching sessions and at the breaking of bread services and prayer meetings" (Acts 2:41, 42, LB).

The early Christians were looked upon as a fellowship or a community, rather than a church. *Church* is a misleading word today, referring to a building for many people and of a fellowship of worshiping people.

Community, according to the Oxford dictionary, is "a body of persons having a community life ... a state, town, school, convent, profession, or *bee-hive!*" Many church fellowships today are rather like bee-hives, with the members continually stinging one another and sometimes the ministers having too many theological "bees in the bonnet."

If the younger generation is to be integrated into the Christian community, which we call the church, then we must return to the four-fold secret of the day of Pentecost when three thousand were added to the church in one day.

Verses 41 to 47 of Acts 2 reveal how they entered the fellowship, exercised their fellowship and expressed their fellowship. Or to put it another way, they had a basis for fellowship, an expression of this fellowship and a secret for maintaining the fellowship.

Let us look at this four-fold secret in detail; it can be summed up in four words: authority, fraternity, ceremony and liturgy.

I. AUTHORITY—"regular attendance at the apostles' teaching" (Acts 2:42).

We are living in days when authority is at a low ebb everywhere. Educational methods are beginning to turn full circle. "Free discipline" (a contradiction in terms!), when every child was allowed to "do his own thing," has now been seen as causing insecurity. Children and young people expect and like a certain amount of discipline in school and in the home. It makes them more secure and mature.

Anarchy has spread into the churches and as Spurgeon once put it when describing a certain sect, "None of us knows anything and we all teach each other." God's "frozen people" need unfreezing, but sometimes they can become too unfrozen and like the period of the Judges, ". . . every man did that which was right in his own eyes" (Judg. 17:6). "Obey them that have the rule over you," wrote Paul, and he urged that "faithful men" should be entrusted with the important task of "teaching others also." One of the gifts of the ascended Lord to the church is pastors and *teachers*.

II. FRATERNITY—"They joined with the other believers" (v. 42).

"Faithful to the brotherhood" is another modern translation of the word "fellowship" in the Authorized or King James Version. In the Acts of the Apostles and the Epistles the word *brother* or *brethren* is used 147 times. Peter's injunction to believers was, "Love the brotherhood." He placed that instruction *before* "fear God." There was obviously a great sense of fraternity in the early church. Like the people of God in Malachi's day, ". . . they that feared the Lord spake often one to another" (Mal. 3:16).

Friendship can be found in clubs and pubs, but New Testament fellowship is something entirely different from friendship, valuable and enjoyable as that may be. The word *fellowship* is the same Greek word that is used in the New Testament for the communion service or Lord's Supper. The "fellowship meal" is where Christian fellowship is realized at its deepest level.

III. CEREMONY—"the breaking of bread services" (v. 42).

Today the sacraments are not central enough in many churches, which is to the detriment of worship and the spiritual life of members. Sometimes there are household communion services and baptisms, instead of them being within the context of the worshiping church. Both sacraments are "acted creeds" and should not be celebrated in isolation or as an appendage to ordinary worship. When the early Christians met on the first day of the week it was to break bread. Prior to that they had broken bread daily. After that they celebrated communion weekly, and beyond that Scripture does not go. Why is it then that some denominations do not hold communion services at all, and others once every quarter? It is no wonder church members have become lax in attendance.

IV. LITURGY—"and in prayer" (v. 42).

The Greek text has "and in *the* prayers," as if there was a set liturgical form of prayer already in existence. For some today prayers that are read are "gabbled through"; for others "free" or extempore prayer is making the Almighty, "all-matey." And so it is difficult to please everyone. Perhaps a compromise is needed: some prayers could be read, and some extemporized. It has been said that if we prepare to speak to man (sermon notes), then we should the more prepare to speak to God, and many ministers who would not read prayers from a book do find it helpful to write out "headline" thoughts for their prayers so that when they lead their congregations in public prayer they do not become repetitive week after week.

Does the church therefore need revival and renewal? Yes, indeed! We need an awakening similar to the eighteenth century and other revivals of history. On the other hand we also need to walk the old paths and get back to the secrets of the early church when three thousand were added to their number in one day, and each day fresh soldiers joined their ranks.

CHAPTER THIRTEEN

WITHOUT NUMBER
Harvest

"... I know not the numbers thereof" (Ps. 71:15).

When the psalmist was speaking about his enemies he could not count them, but he could make a comparison: they "are more than the hairs of mine head" (Ps. 69:4). When he thinks of his daily supply of mercies he can neither calculate nor make a comparison—they are innumerable. If he had lived in our computer age he would have caused the computer to blow a fuse as he fed into the machine the different mercies and blessings he received at God's hand. So, too, as we consider at harvest time the way God has been faithful throughout another year, we have to say, "Transported with the view, I'm lost in wonder, love and praise."

Psalm 71 is entitled by Jewish comentators, "A prayer for old age." It is the song of an old man, still enduring trials, but still trusting in the goodness and generosity of almighty God.

In the same spirit we observe the harvest thanksgiving. After diligent preparation of the soil and the sowing of the seed, we wait for God to give the right weather conditions so that the seed can spring up into life and produce an abundant crop of flowers, fruit and vegetables.

Taking the second half of the text first we note *the number of his mercies*. The Living Bible translation is, "I will tell everyone how good you are, and of your constant daily care." The Good News Bible reads, "They are more than I can understand." They are "past my knowledge" (RSV).

Mercies are the material, temporal gifts of God; blessings are the spiritual (temporal and eternal) tokens of God's bounty. The psalmist does not specify which he means, so we may assume he is thinking of and thanking God for both.

"Count your blessings, name them one by one" goes the chorus. No wonder an evangelist got his congregation to sing, "Name them four by four," and when you've done that "remember there are a million more!"

"Do you count sheep when you can't sleep at night," one Christian asked another. "No, I count my blessings." This is a good idea but an impossible one.

Since we cannot particularize let us generalize:

God's *promises* are incalculable. Feed the promises of the Bible into a computer and various answers have been given as to the total number ranging from 7,487, to 30,000! Since there are only 31,173 verses in the Bible, the latter figure makes almost every verse a promise!

God's *answers to our prayers* are incalculable. There are 650 prayers in the Bible, 450 with recorded answers. On top of that we must compile our own list of prayers, some answered in the affirmative, some in the negative (for He knows what is best for us), and some with answers delayed until the right time.

The old preacher Rowland Hill once sent some money to a poor minister with a note: "There's more to follow." The next month he sent another gift with a note, "More to follow." This he did until a sizeable gift had been sent. He was afraid he might overwhelm the poor minister if he sent it all at once. So there is always more to follow with God; harvest after harvest comes round because of His promise that "seedtime and harvest shall not cease."

Looking at the first half of the text we note *the nature of our gratitude*: "I will tell everyone how good you are . . ." (v. 15, LB).

We may not be able to count or calculate, but we can continually praise Him. This is what the psalmist does in verses 22 to 24. Note that we *sing* to God but *speak* to men. Like Paul, the psalmist knew that it was right to adopt this attitude: "In every thing give thanks" ("Be thankful whatever the circumstances may be" Phillips).

A Chinese fable tells of an old farmer working a tiny plot of land with little yield for his labors. His son wanted him to sell the small holding, but the old man heard that he would be rich if only he would plant trees.

He dug the first hole for the first tree and while doing so uncovered an old urn. He took it indoors and began to clean it with a brush. While doing so it became full of brushes which he sold at the market. While cleaning it again a coin from the sales fell into the urn and the urn became full of coins. As fast as he emptied it, the urn became full of money again. The son shut his father up in the attic to spend his time counting their riches. The father became so weak that he himself fell into the urn and the urn became full of dead bodies. The son had to spend all the money burying the bodies! In the end he was poorer than ever.

During another twelve months God has been filling our urn. Once again He has been pleased to supply our material needs. What is the nature of our gratitude? When we think of the Third World with millions homeless, nearly naked and living on a starvation diet, what form should our gratitude take? The apostle James tells us: "Suppose there are brothers or sisters who need clothes and don't have enough to eat. What good is there in your saying to them 'God bless you! Keep warm and eat well!'—if you don't give them the necessities of life? So it is with faith: if it is alone and includes no actions, then it is dead" (James 2:15-17, GNB). We must support missionaries who go to teach backward nations how to use farming machinery, how to increase the yield of their land and feed the starving. We must pray for those who sow the seed of the gospel, missionaries, pastors and evangelists. One day there will be in heaven "a number which no man can number." Will some be there because of our giving, our praying, our preaching and our witnessing?